Pray and Learn Shapes with
Edgar G. Frog
in the
Forest of Shapes

Written and Illustrated By - Linda D. Washington
Edited By - Rita K. Jeffries

Copyright ©2024 Products and Activities for Christian Education (PACE) LTD

A Prayer for the Children

Father,

You are an Awesome God and Father!
Thank You so much for loving the little children.

We ask in the name of the Lord Jesus that You protect the children everywhere they go. Please let them know that they do not have to be afraid because You are with them. Praise You Abba!

Will You put a reminder of You and Your Love in each child's heart, so they will choose to "always pray," and trust You, Jesus, and Holy Spirit? Thank You Father for always answering our prayers by Jesus. We love You!

Amen (Colossians 4:17)

Story Introduction

Edgar G was a little boy. Everyday Edgar G would pray with his parents before he went to school. His mom and dad told Edgar G to Always Pray and talk to God, our Father in heaven. They told Edgar G that God, Jesus and Holy Spirit would always help him when he prayed.

One day when Edgar G was in school, he did not want to learn about shapes. So, he closed his eyes tight. He fell asleep wishing that he would never have to learn anything. He wanted to hop and play all day. Edgar G dreamed that his school, his teachers, and all his friends had disappeared---POOF! GONE! *And* he was no longer an Edgar G boy *but a funny Edgar G Frog*. Edgar G was lost. To get home he needed help. He had to go through a Forest of Shapes. There were two new friends waiting to help him begin his new adventure in the…

Forest of Shapes

"Hi, I'm Rec-Tangle!"
said the box shaped friend

"And I'm C C Circle!"

Edgar G extended his arm to greet his new friends.

But when he looked at *his green frog arm*, he shouted,

"WOW, I'M GREEN!"

"Are you okay?" *asked CC Circle.*

"What? Oh yes," *Edgar G answered.*
"I am not a frog. I'm really a little boy.
The last thing I remember is being at school and
closing my eyes real tight.
Then **BAM!**
Here I am, a funny green frog.
But you can call me Edgar G."

"Well, well," *said C C Circle,* "It sounds like Jelly Bean to me."

"Jelly Bean? What is Jelly Bean?" *Edgar G asked.*

Rec-Tangle looked around before stuttering, "*He – he - he's* just a junk food eating, bad breathed, jelly bean popping, tickly-toed, pot-bellied dragon, who sneezes every time he eats his favorite candy, *JE – JE - JELLY* BEANS!"

"What does that have to do with me being a frog?" *Edgar G asked.*

"Quite a bit" *C C Circle answered,* "You see my friend, every time the Jelly Bean dragon gobbles up Jelly beans, he sneezes, *and things happen!*"

"Ye – Ye -Yes," *Rec-Tangle agreed,* "Somehow his sneezes get tangled up into a child's wish, then at that precise moment ------ PIZZIT!"

"**Pizit?**" *Edgar G repeated.*

"N – n – NO, *Rec-Tangle stammered*
It's PIZZIT!"

C C Circle explained,
"You see Edgar G, that's the sound we hear when the Jelly Bean dragon sneezes at the same time a child makes a wish. Hmm, did you happen to make a wish?"

"Yes I did," *said Edgar G.*
"I wished I could hop and play all day."

"H – H - Hop and play all day," *said Rec-Tangle,*
"It sounds like your wish got mixed up
with Jelly Bean's sneeze."

Edgar G asked,
"What can I do to become a boy again and go home?"

CC Circle answered,
"I'm not sure, but there is this crazy bird who lives in the Forest of Shapes. Maybe he can tell you how to get home."

"Yippee!" Edgar G shouted as he hopped UP, UP and into the air. Then down he came, landing on a long tree branch.

*"Caw! Caw! Caw!
You're funny!
Caw! Caw! Caw!"*
A bird in the tree was laughing.

Edgar G looked down at his friends.

C C Circle pointed up, towards a bird, standing on the same branch as Edgar G.

Big tears ran down the bird's face as he rocked back and forth laughing.

**He stopped laughing *when*
he lost his balance
AND . . .**

...FELL TO THE GROUND!

Everyone watched as the crazy bird
jumped to his feet.
He brushed off his jacket.

He adjusted his suspenders and pointed to
himself saying,
"I'm Buzzy!"

Buzzy rubbed his hands together and
motioned for Edgar G to come closer.

Edgar G thought,
"What should I do? I'm afraid!"

He remembered his parents and how they told him to
ALWAYS PRAY to heavenly Father and to ***TRUST Jesus***!

So Edgar G prayed *quietly* **inside of himself.**

As he prayed, Edgar G remembered that Jesus said,
"Don't be afraid."
Jesus will never leave us.
Jesus is with us when we are in trouble.
Edgar G smiled.
He knew *that he could be brave.*
Jesus was with him.
So, he hopped to the ground near Buzzy.

Edgar G asked,
"Did you say your name was Buzzy?"

"Yep! Sure did,"
replied the crazy bird.
"Caw! Caw!"
"What's your problem little frog?"

Edgar G asked,
"Can you help me find my way home and become a boy again?"

Buzzy poked out his chest and pulled on his suspenders until . . . . **POP!**

Buzzy soared through the air.

He grabbed a tree.
His legs and coat tails flapped in the wind.

Buzzy poked his head around the tree and said,
"I can tell you about the Shape Forest!"

Edgar G hopped closer.

Buzzy pointed to a path leading into the forest and said,
"Follow the path,
heh, heh, heh, CAW!"

Edgar G asked,
**"Will that path lead me home
so I can become a boy again?"**

Buzzy crowed,
"CAW! Remember this!
The forest before you have shapes inside,
some round, some square, some oval.
Name the shape on the leaf,
it takes your belief,
to get you through Jelly Bean's forest."

"Oh my," *said Edgar G,*
as his little green body slowly sank to the ground.

"Wh – Wh – Why are you so sad my friend?"
asked Rec-Tangle.

Edgar G said, **"I did not always pay attention when my parents and teacher showed me shapes."**

C C Circle asked,
"Do you know the names of any shapes?"

Edgar G said,
"I know that you are round….and round is shaped like a … oh, what is it called?"

Edgar G paused.

He was not certain.
He whispered the words, ***"a circle."***

Buzzy asked,
"What did you say?"

Edgar G was quiet.

Edgar G said,
"I NEED TO PRAY! God will help me!"

So, Edgar G prayed again.

He said:
"Father,
I am not afraid to do this, but I need Your help.
Will You help me remember the shapes I learned?
I know You will help me.
Jesus and Holy Spirit always help me
when I ask you Father!

Thank You!
Amen!"

His friends said, **"YOU CAN DO IT EDGAR G!
And when you want to learn a new shape,**
ask someone who knows!"

Edgar G *knew* **that God was with him.
So, before he hopped,** *he said,*
"Thank You Father!
Thank You Jesus!
Thank You Holy Spirit!"

And with great confidence Edgar G shouted,
"CIRCLE!"
as he hopped onto the first circle shape.

Memory Verses to Teach Children

Always Pray and Never Give Up

Luke 18:1

Do not be afraid because I am with you

Isaiah 41:10

Prayer Song to Teach Children

(Sung to the tune of the "Up on the Housetop" chorus)

"You can pray, do it today.
You can pray, do it today.

Pray to Father, He's waiting for you.
He will tell you what to do."

Forest of Shapes
Pray and Learn Shapes
Game Instructions

Before beginning the game, carefully cut out the Edgar G Frog game pieces; the game cards; and game sheet at the back of this book. To stand the game piece up after cutting fold it on the crease.

1) AT THE BEGINNING OF THE GAME SAY:
God wants us to PRAY AT ALL TIMES!
We can pray and talk to God about anything.
Let's pray before we play.

2) LET EACH CHILD WHO WANTS TO PRAY DO SO.
If no one chooses to pray, an adult (as an example) can say a brief prayer to our heavenly Father and end the prayer by thanking Father. (Remind the children who prayed to thank God after they pray)

TO PLAY The Forest Of Shapes
Number of Players: 2

3) DECIDE WHO WANTS TO PLAY FIRST AND SECOND.
Choose a colored Edgar G. Frog game piece and place on the game sheet by the feet of Edgar G Frog.

4) MIX THE CARDS
Place the cards in a stack with the frog-side face down within reach of both players.

5) EACH PLAYER IN TURN
a. Pull the top card.
b. Follow the arrows and hop their playing piece the number of spaces indicated on the card.
c. Name the shape landed on. IF THE CHILD DOES NOT KNOW THE SHAPE YET, THEY CAN ASK SOMEONE WHO KNOWS.

6) WHEN A PLAYER LANDS ON THE JELLY-BEAN DRAGON OR BUZZY SPACE
The player gets to pull another card and move ahead the number of frogs on the card.

7) WINNING THE GAME
Going through the Forest of Shapes is achieved by pulling a card that would take the player beyond the last shape.

8) IF ALL CARDS ARE USED AND THE PLAYERS HAVE NOT GONE BEYOND THE LAST SHAPE:
Mix the cards and stack them. Then use the cards over again.

Playing Pieces

Cut the playing pieces along the color lines to separate them. After the four playing pieces are separated, fold the bottom of the playing piece along the white dotted line to stand the piece up on the game sheet.
Extra playing pieces are included.
Option: Use different objects as playing pieces, such as a button and a rock, etc.

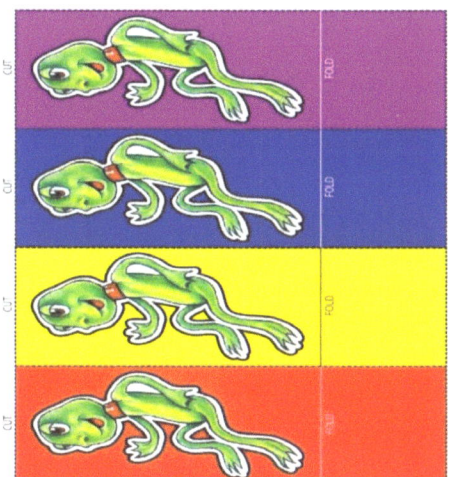 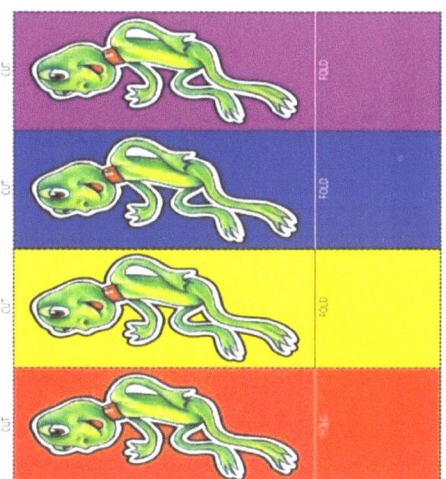

Recommended: After cutting to separate the playing pieces, keep all of the game parts, which includes, the playing pieces, cards and game sheet in a zip lock type bag,

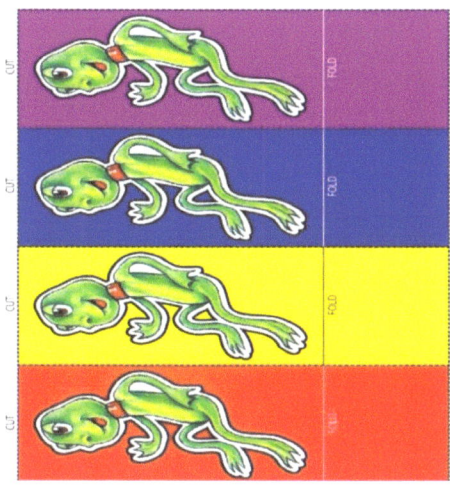 

GAME CARDS
Sheet 1 of 2
Cut cards out along the lines

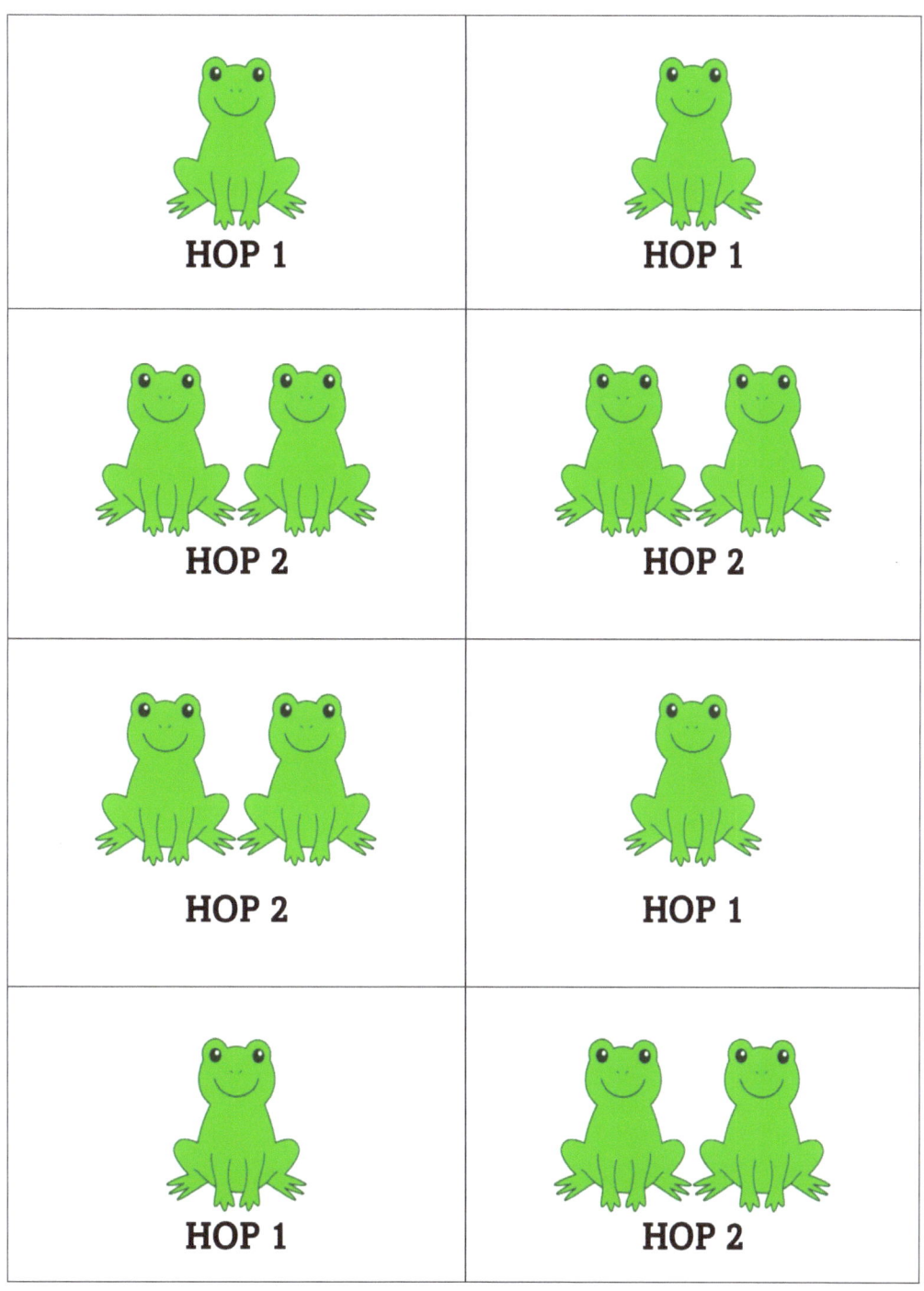

GAME CARDS
Sheet 2 of 2
Cut cards out along the lines

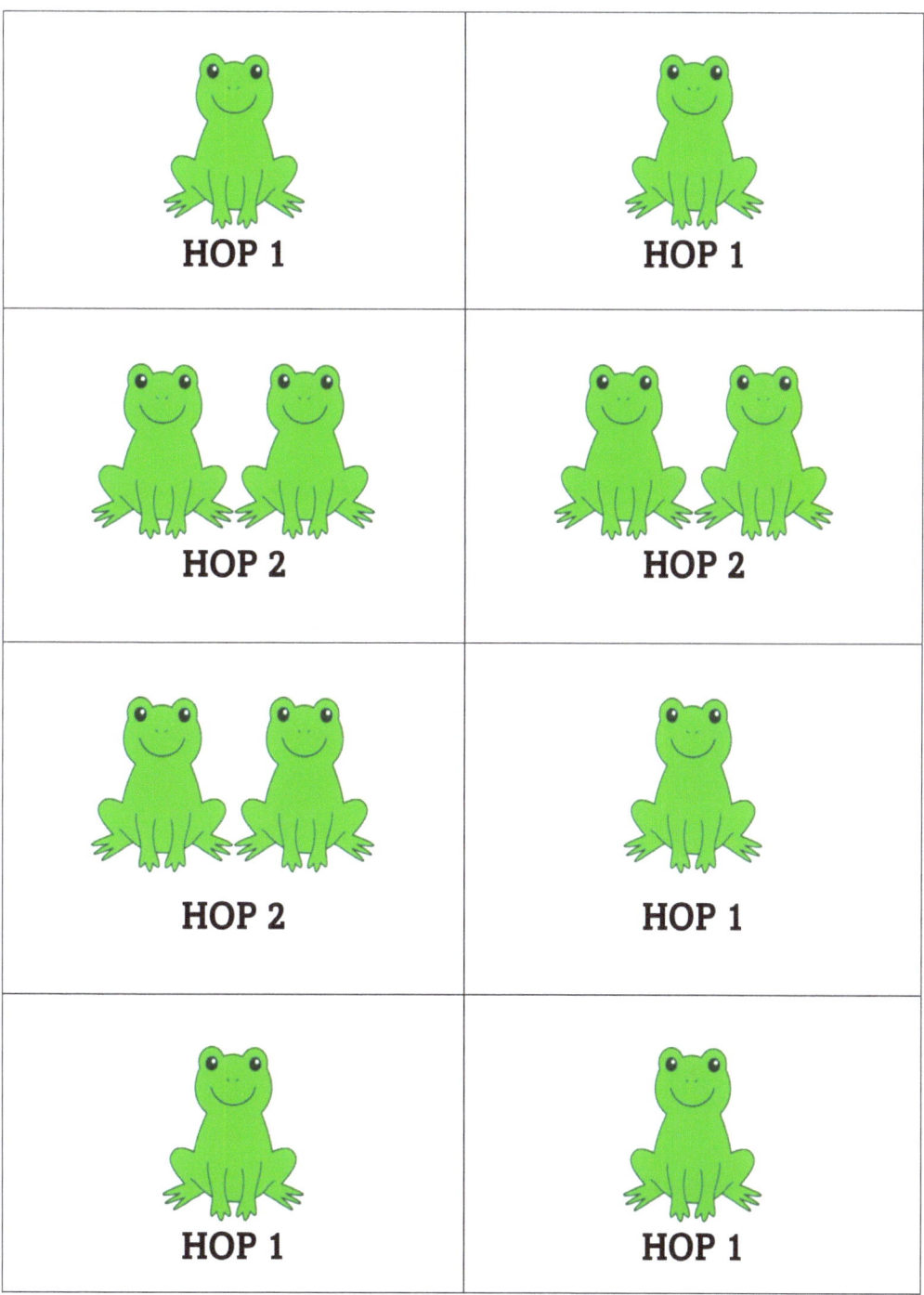

Forest of Shapes
Game Sheet

www.ingramcontent.com/pod-product-compliance
Lightning Source LLC
LaVergne TN
LVHW072114070426
835510LV00002B/41